NOW YOU CAN REA...............

ANIMALS IN DANGER

TEXT BY KAREN GOAMAN

ILLUSTRATED BY DAVID THOMPSON

BRIMAX BOOKS · NEWMARKET · ENGLAND

Many kinds of animals are in danger. They may become extinct. This means they die out and not one is left. People are often to blame. They hunt and kill some animals. Some farmers shoot big bears to keep them away from their own animals.

People sell the skins and furs of the animals they hunt. Rhinos are hunted for their horns.

People also change the places where animals live. Giant pandas are found in the bamboo forests of China. The trees are cut down to build towns. The pandas have nowhere to live and nothing to eat.

Some big cats are in danger because they are hunted by people.

Tigers live in cool mountain areas or hot forests in Asia. For many years hunters have killed tigers for sport.

The clouded leopard has markings on its coat. Why do you think this big cat is hunted?

Jaguars live in the forests of South and Central America. You can see that many trees in this forest were cut down. This is to make space for farming.

Monkeys and apes live in jungles. They may lose their homes in the trees.

This black ape is a gorilla. It is a large animal but it is gentle.

This monkey is an aye-aye. It uses its long middle finger to dig out food.

Look at the orang-utan. It has shaggy red hair.

These monkeys live in Brazil. The uakari (*wakari*) has a red face. The other monkeys are golden lion tamarins.

Years ago, there were lots of wolves. Now they live in only a few places. They were killed for their fur.

Mongolian wild horses are the only wild horses left. They are very shy.

The rock wallaby and the koala live in Australia. Look for the rings on the wallaby's tail. The baby koala clings to its mother's back. These animals were hunted for their skins. Now there are laws to stop the hunting.

Giant otters and manatees are hunted by people in the American rivers where they live. Manatees are killed for meat and otters for their fur. Look at the giant otter's feet.

Monk seals eat fish. Fishermen kill the seals because they want to catch the fish.

Here is a blue
whale. Only
a few hundred
are left. Look at
the size of it!
Whales are killed
for their meat
and their fat.
Whale fat is called blubber.

Here are some
reptiles in danger
of dying out.

This crocodile is found in India.
Look at its long narrow snout.
Its teeth are like needles.
People take its eggs for food.

Turtles are killed
for their meat and
shells. Their eggs
are taken too.

The tuatara of New Zealand is hunted for food. Do you think it looks like a dinosaur?

This is a Fijian banded iguana. There are only a few left. Their eggs are eaten by mongooses.

The San Francisco garter snake lives in marshes. People drained many marshes to build on the land.

Many birds of prey are in danger because they are hunted for sport.

There are only about 40 of these birds left. They are California condors. Look at the bird's huge bill and bald head.

This bird is called the monkey-eating eagle. Can you see why? It lives in Asian forests.

Some birds of prey are dying out because chemicals stop their eggs hatching. These chemicals are sprayed on to crops and washed into the sea by rainwater. The birds take in the chemicals when they eat fish. Look for the bald eagle's yellow bill and white head. The other bird is an osprey.

People hunt and kill whooping cranes. They also drain and dig up the marshes where the cranes live.

These New Zealand birds do not fly. They cannot escape from cats and dogs. The kakapo lives in forests. The takahe is found near water.

These birds of paradise are hunted
for their very pretty feathers.
The males show off their feathers.

The red iwi lives
in Hawaii. People
use its feathers
to make clothes
for the chief.

The world's largest butterfly is
Queen Alexandra's birdwing. It is
bigger than your foot. The big
grasshopper is a giant weta of
New Zealand. It is eaten by rats.

The great raft
spider is found
in England.
There is only
one marsh where
it lives.

These animals on the sea bed are taken for their meat and shells. Look for the green giant clams. These are eaten by people. The shell of the triton is used as a trumpet.

The huge coconut crab lives on land in the Pacific Ocean. It is killed for people to eat.

You have read about many animals in danger. Here are some more. Can you find out why these animals are dying out?

Ocelot

Everglade kite

Woolly spider monkey

Alligator